How to Defend the Faith

a presuppositional approach

By Riley Fraas

To my wife.

Table of Contents

Chapter I. Introduction – the role of apologetics in the gospel conversation

A. What is apologetics?

The word: *Apologetics* may not be entirely familiar to most Christians. What does it mean? Apologetics is a defense of the faith. It has nothing to do with apologizing. The word *apologetics* comes from the Greek word "apologia" meaning defense. What is in view is not a confessional, but a shield. This particular type of shield known as *Apologetics* is an intellectual shield to deflect the darts that fly at the Christian who is debating an unbeliever. The objections of the unbeliever tend to focus on topics from the basic doctrines of Christianity, to the Bible, the morality of both, etc. The thoughtful Christian would like to have an intelligent response handy to deflect such objections that unbelievers make, and this is the field of Apologetics. Apologetics is not always necessary. One can share the gospel without using apologetics, but there are times when apologetics is a useful tool to continue a conversation and steer it back to the gospel, which is the goal. In the sport of fencing, there is a parry and a riposte (an offensive attack after a successful defensive block called the "parry".) Apologetics is the conversational parry and the gospel is the riposte. One defends against objections with apologetics, and attacks the heart with the gospel. One can imagine a conversation going like this:

Unbeliever: "Why do you believe in all this Christianity stuff?"

Christian: "I believe in Christ because he is God come in the flesh to save sinners like you and me."

Unbeliever: "Bah, that's just stupid. Why would

you believe such a thing?"

Christian: "Holy men of God were eyewitnesses of His power, death, resurrection, and ascension back to heaven. The Holy Spirit guided them to write down the record of who Christ is with complete credibility and accuracy."

Unbeliever: "I don't believe that. What evidence can you show me to convince me that it's true?"

At this point, the Christian has a choice to make. He can simply continue to proclaim the good news of Jesus Christ boldly as it is revealed in Scripture. He can say something like this:

Christian: "God has given you all the evidence you need that He exists in nature, and He's sent His own Son to offer mercy and peace to you, if you will repent of your sins and submit your mind to Christ. He will soon come again to judge the living and the dead. Repent and believe now before it's too late! Read the Bible for yourself, and come to church with me where you will hear it proclaimed and taught obediently, and you will see the credibility and truthfulness of these testimonies written in it, if the Lord opens your eyes to believe."

There's absolutely nothing wrong with the above approach. The situation will dictate whether it is most appropriate to simply and biblically proclaim gospel truth vs. parrying the counterarguments and objections of the unbeliever in great detail. Times to take this approach, of merely presenting the good news without answering possible objections, would be when the conversation is very short. When I was the chaplain at the Kit Carson Correctional Center in Burlington, Colorado, on the eastern plains, once a week I would spend a half hour in conversation and prayer with up to 52 inmates in the special housing unit. I only had a minute or two to talk to each one including listening to prayer requests, providing counsel, answering questions, and taking requests for Bibles and other books from my library. In this situation, time would sometimes restrict me to proclaiming the gospel one on one, without answering every conceivable intellectual objection, stated or not. The Christian layman will likewise find himself in situations in which he is giving some quick or parting words to a friend, relative, or complete stranger. In these types of situations the priorities to communicate are the law that brings the knowledge of sin and/or the gospel of salvation in Christ through repentance from sin and faith in Him.

The law comes before the gospel. The bad

news must come before the good news. As the sparkle of a cut diamond is best seen against the backdrop of black cloth, so the light of the gospel shines most brightly when the sinner's sinful and miserable condition is understood. (The state of heart of the person with whom one is talking will determine whether they are yet in need of being broken by the law before they can be healed by the gospel. Sometimes the law that breaks the pride of man is all that can be communicated, and the gospel will have to wait until the weight of the law sinks in deeply.) On the other hand, there are times when not responding to the particular worldview of the unbeliever in a specific way will unnecessarily cut off the conversation and limit future opportunities to share the good news. When the unbeliever has a particular objection or request that must be answered in order to continue the conversation in hopes of steering it back to the gospel, a defense of the faith against his particular objection or worldview: an *apologetic,* will be a handy tool in the arsenal of the Christian. One could imagine the conversation continuing like this:

Unbeliever: "What evidence can you show me that your God is the true God?"

Christian: "Well, for starters, all existing evidence points to the Trinitarian God of Scripture, because He made everything that exists. Let's take you for example. You are evidence for the existence of the Trinitarian God of Scripture."

Unbeliever: "[Chuckles] Huh? I don't even believe in your God. How am I evidence for Him?"

Christian: "Because you asked me for

evidence, showing a tendency for logic, in that your rational mind is unlikely to accept a conclusion that is without rational proof or evidence. Rationality is a product of the mind of the Trinitarian God. Since He made you, your mind tends to use reason. This rationality reflects His rational mind. When you ask for evidence, you borrow from the biblical Christian worldview, but only when the situation absolutely requires."

Unbeliever: "I do no such thing! I'm not a believer in your God."

Christian: "Well, if it's true as you say, that you're not selectively borrowing from biblical Christianity when you ask for evidence, then please kindly give a rational account for, (that is, offer an explanation for,) the existence of laws of logic that allow you to proceed from evidence to a conclusion."

Unbeliever: "Um, well, it's just the way my mind works."

Christian: "Exactly, and since you can't explain why your mind works that way, given your view of the universe and the origins of your mind, I'm correct to assert that you're borrowing from biblical Christianity when you ask for evidence. If it were not for the Trinitarian God of Scripture having created you and your mind, you wouldn't and couldn't ask for evidence. But it does show that your worldview, whatever it is, is irrational, since it can't even explain the origin and existence of basic facts about our reality that you know intuitively, namely, the existence of laws of logic. Repent of your irrational unbelieving worldview and embrace Christ as He is revealed in the Holy Scriptures. Then you will discover true rationality."

So what has just happened in this imaginary conversation? The Christian answered the question of the unbeliever who asked for evidence, in a way that led back to a presentation of the gospel. Unlike the conversation noted above, where the Christian did not answer the unbeliever's question at all, this time he answered it in a way that helped the Christian to steer it back to the good news of Jesus Christ, the Savior of all those who repent and believe in Him. In football, Apologetics is the block that sets up the gospel rush to the outside for a first down. This *parry* that sets up the next gospel *riposte*, to use the fencing analogy, is the element of this conversation that keeps it going so that the Christian can share the gospel.

This is what Apologetics is, what it does, and how to use it.

B. The Presuppositional Apologetic

The Argument: *The existence of the Trinitarian God of Scripture is proven by the rational impossibility of the contrary.*

This is the formal claim made by the presuppositional Apologist. It is a conclusion that will have to be demonstrated. There are other approaches or apologetic arguments, from Thomas Aquinas's theistic proofs, Anselm's ontological proof for God, or more recent evidentialist approaches such as those made by Josh McDowell and Lee Strobel. Those types of arguments are not what we are utilizing in this handbook. The presuppositional apologetic was pioneered by the twentieth century professor at Westminster Theological Seminary named Cornelius Van Til. His apologetic brought a new awareness to the presuppositions, those foundational assumptions that govern and provide a framework for all of your thinking. It is impossible to think without presuppositions. The arrangement of chairs around a table presupposes a stable floor. Both presuppose laws of physics that allow for bodies to remain stationary. The atoms that make up the floor and the chairs are not going to spontaneously combust or separate into globs of goo heading in opposite directions. There are basic facts about physics in our reality that must be presupposed in order to think about how to arrange the chairs around a table. Usually we do not even think about these things. The presuppositional apologetic takes nothing for granted. Every presupposition must be examined rationally to see if it fits within the stated philosophical worldview of the one in the debate. He will not be allowed to unthinkingly presuppose things that his philosophical worldview cannot explain or account for. In that case he is relying on data and propositions that his view of the universe does not give him the right to use. Since people just ordinarily and unthinkingly presuppose many things in ordinary life that they know naturally without study, by intuition, not by deductive logic processed through their brain, it will take some work to help them understand the argument. They ordinarily just assume the chairs are going to stay on the floor without giving a second thought to how they depend on the law of gravity. People are not used to thinking about these things. Since the one with whom the Christian is having a conversation will perhaps have never encountered the presuppositional argument before, he will not be accustomed to identifying, let alone examining, his own presuppositions in the light of his own stated worldview. So the first task of the Christian apologist must be to help the one with whom he is in a conversation to recognize the presuppositions that govern his own thought.

1. The rationale for this type of apologetic

a. The futility of the autonomous observer demonstrated by Kant

Classical apologetics is made up of the common arguments for the existence of God famously propounded by Thomas Aquinas and Anselm. It was taught in all schools of Christian doctrine including the theological seminaries and academies in the Reformed tradition from the Reformation to many of them in this day. It relies heavily on Aristotelian philosophy.

Aristotle, the ancient classical Greek philosopher, discovered many things about the reality of our universe by his keen intellect and powers of observation. But his philosophical worldview could not quite account for the existence of the things that he observed in nature, since it was a closed system featuring an "Unmoved Mover" as the first cause, but who was not separate and distinct from the universe that we inhabit[1], which according to Aristotle is eternally preexistent. Immanuel Kant, an eighteenth century Prussian philosopher, in his *Critique of Pure Reason,* made a ground-breaking discovery: that left to himself, the philosopher is entirely dependent upon his five senses[2] and his own mind. He can only know and think on what his senses tell him, or what his reason presents to him. He cannot actually be sure whether his senses are transmitting objectively accurate information to him about the reality around him. He also cannot know whether his reason is presenting ideas to him that are objectively true outside of his own consciousness. Without an external point of reference, he is left in a prison of subjectivity. He can only live by what the senses and his individual reason tell him without knowing whether it is

---

[1] Karl Holzamer, *Philosophie,* Guetersloh: Bertelsmann Verlag, 1961, 204.
[2] Holzamer, 270.

accurate or not, like Neo in the movie *The Matrix* before he swallowed the pill that woke him up from his imaginary dream world. By pointing out the subjectivity of man's sensory perception, Kant's critique devastates the idea that man can objectively know anything at all independently of God.

Van Til responded to Kant by pointing out that the self-revelation of the Trinitarian God of Christianity, in the form of the written text of the Holy Scriptures, provides the external point of reference[3] that allows the thinking man to know something objectively about the reality around him. While the unbeliever is trapped in a prison of subjectivity, relying only on his own sensory perception, the Christian has an upper hand. He can know that his understanding of reality is accurate as far as his powers of observation and interpretation allow, because the Bible teaches him

---

[3] Cornelius Van Til, *The Defense of the Faith*, Phillipsburg, NJ: Presbyterian and Reformed Publishing Co., 1955, 180.

that there is a rational God who created him to think His thoughts after Him, to know and discover things about reality, glorifying the Creator for His creation. While classical and evidentialist approaches to apologetics invite the unbeliever to see how the facts of reality point to the existence of God, or the resurrection of Christ, etc., the presuppositional approach deals with the problem of the inability of man to know anything as it is apart from its relation to its Creator, the objective external reference that makes accurate observation possible for man.

b. The Impact of Sin on man's powers of thought and observation

The Bible reveals that God created man as His image and reflection, to think His thoughts after Him. By disobedience to God's command not to eat of the tree of the knowledge of good and evil,

Adam and Eve rebelled against their Creator, seeking to be autonomous, that is, independent observers and interpreters of the reality around them. They sought intellectual and moral independence from their Creator. The serpent said, "Hath God said, ye shalt not eat of any tree in the garden…Ye shall not surely die: For God doth know that in the day that ye eat thereof, then your eyes shall be opened, and ye shall be as gods, knowing good and evil." (Genesis 3:1-5) The sin of Adam and Eve, in succumbing to the temptation of the serpent, was in wishing to be autonomous observers, interpreters, and indeed determiners of reality. They wanted to be independent from God in their thoughts and destinies. Like *Pinocchio*, who wanted to be a real boy, they wished to be something they were not. They wanted to be creators instead of creatures.

This sinful train of thought continues today for the unbeliever. He thinks that he is able by his own powers of reason, observation, and interpretation to come to a correct knowledge about himself and his reality apart from any reference to his Creator. He wants to know things about reality without honoring God or depending upon His revealed interpretation to shape and correct his thinking about it. This is the false presupposition that colors the unbeliever's interpretation of the evidence for God. When the unbeliever says, "show me the evidence", he is in effect proclaiming himself free, independent, and autonomous of YHWH[4] his Creator. He is judging himself competent to put God on trial and examine the evidence for Him as to its credibility. His non-Christian worldview is in this way assumed from the start. By starting off presupposing that he is competent to examine natural evidence for or against the existence of YHWH, he shows that he believes himself to be

---

[4] YHWH is the covenant name for God in Hebrew given in Genesis and used throughout the Old Testament, ordinarily translated "LORD" in English Bibles.

independent of Him. Whether or not he believes will not impact his interpretation. He is perfectly competent to examine and interpret the evidence apart from YHWH. This assumes YHWH does not exist, because, as the Christian knows, man is a creature of God dependent on Him for everything. He can only rightfully be certain that he is interpreting nature correctly if his thoughts are lining up with the LORD's thoughts. Since he does not concern Himself with YHWH at all from the start, but assumes the question of the existence of Him is irrelevant to his ability to observe and interpret nature, in effect he is presupposing YHWH does not exist. (Because he could only be competent as an independent interpreter and observer if there were in fact no YHWH.) His presupposition is non-Christian, and it is self-fulfilling. He concludes YHWH does not exist because he starts out by presupposing there is no YHWH. So, naturally, then, whatever evidence comes to his senses, whether historical, biological, or logical, his unbelieving, non-Christian presuppositional framework colors his interpretation, so that the entire thought process leads to a non-Christian conclusion. Sinful man is in rebellion against God since the fall, asserting his autonomy over and against the authority of his Creator. This colors his thinking so that no kind or amount of evidence will lead him to the conclusion that the God of the Bible is the true God. His entire thought process is invested in reaching a contrary conclusion. If YHWH exists, then his entire way of thinking is wrong. He incorrectly assumes that he is an autonomous observer, an independent thinker, able to interpret the facts around him without help from the LORD. But this is nothing else than disbelief in YHWH, for man could only be independent of YHWH if He did not exist. The Christian apologist must challenge his presupposition of personal autonomy, which is nothing but sinful rebellion. It is a denial of the existence of YHWH. The Christian apologist confronts this rebellious thinking. This confrontation will get to the root of the matter, and provide an opportunity to present the gospel, instead of getting bogged down in presenting evidence that the unbeliever will simply misinterpret based on his false presupposition of intellectual autonomy, like discussions of the fossil record or debates about the history of the kingdom of Egypt. It is precisely that presupposition of intellectual autonomy that the Apologist must confront and challenge.

2. The point of contact

a. The innate knowledge everyone has of God from creation

If the thinking of man is dead set against his Creator from the start, how is the presuppositional argument going to connect with his thinking in order to present a credible and challenging alternative way of thinking? It is important for us to remember that man, though fallen in sin, is yet created after God's image, and that this image has not been totally erased in him. There is an innate knowledge of God that continues in man despite all his protests and calculated thinking to the contrary. When the apologist presents an alternative way of thinking, one that makes rational sense of reality, one that takes God at His word and conforms every thought to His, he is presenting a Christian theistic view of reality that the unbeliever already *intuitively* knows to be true.

The Bible teaches us that man knows there is a God, and that His signature is written in creation, but that he "holds" this truth in unrighteousness. (Romans 1:18-21) In psychology they call this denial an example of self-serving bias[5] regarding his Creator. He denies truth that he knows to be true because he finds himself under the judgment of God, and that puts him in danger. He would rather not admit it to himself. But he denies it inconsistently, because whenever he makes use of anything in God's creation, he implicitly affirms His existence and attributes. Otherwise he would not be able to live and get along in God's created reality. So, for example, when sinful man solves an addition problem, he assumes constant and universal laws of Mathematics, which is based on the presupposition of God the Creator who sustains the universe in an orderly way. This innate yet suppressed knowledge provides a point

[5] Myers, David, *Social Psychology*, 11th ed. New York: McGraw-Hill, 2013, 61.

of contact for the apologist who is affirming the reality, existence, and self-revelation of the Creator. He presents the only true worldview to someone who claims another view, but the one who claims the unbelieving worldview intuitively knows that he inhabits a reality created by God. His inner self is conscious of the existence of YHWH from its creation, despite all his protests to the contrary. This point of contact will provide an avenue for him to reconsider and change his thinking, if the Lord wills to change it.

3. The procedure

a. You can literally argue from anything, because everything that exists points to God.

One of the great advantages of the presuppositional apologetic is that you can literally argue from anything that exists. In this handbook,

I will attempt to cover all of the broad categories of thought which would allow the one defending the faith to use literally anything in God's creation to prove His existence and the authenticity of his self-revelation in Holy Scripture. It is crucial to note that in this procedure, we have no interest in proving a general concept of a creator god, a blank which can be filled by the Bible. This would result in a deity similar to Aristotle's "Unmoved Mover." The procedure of presuppositional apologetics argues for the proof of the existence of YHWH the Trinitarian God of the Holy Bible: Father, Son, and Holy Spirit, as He is revealed in the Scripture. It does this right from the start, and not by building up from more general theistic concepts. The idea is to lead up conversationally to a presentation of the authentic gospel of the true God, not to turn atheists into non- Christian believers in a god, like Deists or Unitarians, still dead in their sins and headed to eternal torment in hell.

Since YHWH the Trinitarian God of Scripture created everything that exists, it all points to Him. The Apologist can freely and confidently allow the Unbeliever to choose the topic of conversation and what evidence to discuss. You can start with the unbeliever's snarky criticism of the morality of the Bible, or with his insolent questioning of God's providence in the calamities that befall man in this valley of tears called life: cancer, typhoons, earthquakes, horrible crimes against humanity, and such things. All of these things point to the God of the Bible, because He does His will in all that happens. You can start with facts of biology, chemistry, physics, mathematics, and so on. The unbeliever intuitively knows many things about God's creation from observation and education, even though his worldview would not logically allow for them to exist. A disconnect is revealed between the intuitive knowledge the unbeliever has about things by observation, and the worldview he claims to hold. The Apologist can use this disconnect to challenge the unbeliever's irrational presuppositions. Allow the unbeliever to raise objections, and take them on one at a time.

Often the unbeliever unpracticed in these kinds of discussions will soon run out of intelligent things to say, and simply begin to insult or make strings of bare assertions unsupported by any fact or evidence. That is when the Apologist, if he has made himself understood clearly enough, knows that his argument has reached its point of contact, and that the unbeliever is grasping aimlessly for something to say. Then is the time to pivot to a presentation of the law and gospel, to proclaim judgment to come, and if possible, offer forgiveness in Christ on condition of faith and repentance from sin.

1. The failure of all philosophical worldviews other than biblical Christianity to account for the existence of a diverse universe governed by constant, universal laws.

No comprehensive understanding of the universe, its origin and purpose, can give a rational explanation for the existence of the universe as we know it to be, other than the religion of the Bible. Another way to say that is that non-Christian worldviews cannot *account for* anything as we know it to be in our reality. To *account for* is more than just an affirmation that something is observed to exist. I can say that there are big juicy unpeeled oranges in a bowl on the table in the dining area in our house, but it does not mean that I understand what they are in relation to the whole of reality, what their meaning or significance is, or have a plausible and rational explanation for how they got there starting from the origin of all things. Unless I can provide an explanation that answers for all of that, I don't really know anything at all about the round orange things my eyes tell me are in a bowl on the table. The unbeliever cannot be allowed to simply assert that things exist without providing a comprehensive rational explanation for how they can exist and to what purpose, in his stated worldview. When he does that, he should be reminded that he is selectively borrowing from a biblical Christian worldview, the only framework that provides a rational account for them. And since he will never be able to do that with rational and logical consistency, it is thus demonstrated that he has an irrational worldview that is incapable of accounting for basic facts of reality like the oranges in the bowl on my dining table. He cannot explain how he knows for certain that there are oranges in a bowl on the table in a way that is consistent with his commitment to the autonomy of his reason, to intellectual independence. He intuitively knows they are there, but he cannot prove it in any rational argument that is based on his worldview.

That incapability to account for things proves his worldview to be false, and Christianity's ability to account for everything in reality, proves it to be true. That is the use of the phrase *account for* in the presuppositional apologetic.

By going along in life assuming many things contrary to his stated presupposition, the unbeliever constantly affirms the existence of the Trinitarian God of Scripture. When he makes use of the laws of physics, of logic, or of mathematics, he is using something that only Christianity accounts for, which means that he is in effect borrowing from the biblical Christian worldview. The only explanation that can account for the phenomenon that the unbeliever must borrow from biblical Christianity, is that biblical Christianity is reality. The existence and attributes of the Trinitarian God of Scripture are thus proven by the necessity that the unbeliever must borrow from the concept of the universe revealed in the

Holy Scriptures in order to get by living in it.
This does not suggest that the unbeliever has read
the Bible, although some have. It means simply
that by intuitive observation, through trial and
error, he has figured out that the way to get by in
life is to frequently and selectively make
assumptions that are in fact the same assumptions
that one would have if one had read and believed
the Bible. The only logical explanation for this
phenomenon is that the God of the Bible is God in
reality.

1. A Survey of Popular Worldviews

Before we give examples and instructions on
how to use the presuppositional apologetic in real
dialogue with unbelievers, it is helpful to survey
the various categories of worldviews that prevail in
our world today in contrast to and opposition to
biblical Christianity. Nearly all of the views one
will encounter in conversation will fit into one of

the following categories.

Sometimes the unbeliever will hold to a worldview unthinkingly without claiming to adhere to any worldview in particular. In this case the Christian apologist will have to listen carefully to determine what the worldview of the unbeliever is, in order to respond to it. At other times the unbeliever will make explicit claims to a particular philosophical worldview. Sometimes the unbeliever will play devil's advocate by arguing a view that he does not actually hold to, like when an atheist (irrationally) suggests that there are many gods with as valid a claim as YHWH, effectively making a polytheist and not an atheist argument, with the intent of undercutting the claim that only YHWH is God. Each distinct objection must be answered individually. Now let us proceed to a survey of existing worldviews. The worldview of liberal Christianity will not be addressed, as it tends toward polytheism, pantheism, atheism, or all of the above.

a. Atheism—naturalistic materialism

While atheists are still a tiny minority worldwide, there is a moderately growing number of those who claim belief in no god, particularly in North America and Europe. There is a militant strain in recent years promulgated by Richard Dawkins and his co-believers in atheism that seeks to proselytize the supposedly uninformed toward their irrational point of view. Much more prevalent is the de facto atheism of those who go through life, education, and work unthinkingly as if there is no God. While they must selectively borrow from biblical Christianity to function even minimally in this world, they are not self-consciously aware that they are doing so, and they do not intentionally glorify God in their thoughts about anything.

While some atheists, whether of the self-conscious or *de facto* kind, believe in the supernatural, the majority are what we would describe as materialistic naturalists. They believe that the physical universe made up of matter and energy constitutes the whole of reality, and that natural processes offer the only available explanation for anything that is able to be explained. This is the most irrational worldview of all, for it falls the farthest short of explaining anything in our observed reality. The atheistic materialistic naturalist will often try to conflate natural science with naturalism, as if the natural sciences and the scientific method that governs human observation of them were somehow in agreement with the erroneous philosophical worldview that suggests natural science is the only source of knowledge available to man. Francis Bacon, the devout Puritan Christian and seventeenth century pioneer of the scientific method begged to differ! The naturalistic presupposition of this kind of unbeliever is a convenient shelter from the interpretation that any evidence for the supernatural could even be considered. It dismisses from the start that which it seeks to disprove, providing a convenient self-fulfilling conclusion, like an ostrich with his head in the sand. By only accepting natural evidence and natural explanations for them, the atheist views anything presented through atheistic spectacles. The atheist concludes atheism in a self-fulfilling process that begins with presupposing that only the natural (nothing divine) exists. This is a form of circular reasoning that does not account for reality as we know it. The Apologist will find a lot of material to use to confront the atheist's fallacious presupposition of autonomous reason early on in the conversation. Key intellectual problems with this worldview are its utter lack of even attempting to explain the origin of the universe, or anything about reality that is not measurable through empirical means (that of natural scientific observation.)

b. Pantheism—Hinduism, Buddhism, modern spirituality

Pantheism is a view that suggests that the universe as a whole is a kind of eternal, uncreated, creative, infinite, unconscious, and impersonal power. It is a form of theism, believing that the universe is god, though many who claim to not believe in any gods will hold to it, particularly in the western world where theism is traditionally associated with Christianity, Judaism, or Islam which posit personal gods. Popular forms of explicit pantheism include Hinduism and most branches of Buddhism. When I traveled in India years ago in a predominantly Hindu region, I encountered the phrase: "god is one" in conversation with people about God, and on bumper stickers and window decals on trucks and taxis. "God is one" to a Hindu pantheist means that the entire universe is god. It is one big system.

As hot and cold in a closed system can exist temporarily in parallel, so good and evil, rich and poor, joy and suffering, are two sides of the same coin coexisting as part of this great organism that is the divine everything. The most common Hindi greeting "Namaste" with prayerfully clasped hands acknowledges the divinity of the person that one is greeting. In India, the Christians prefer the greeting, "Salam", meaning peace, an Arabic derivative related to the Hebrew greeting "Shalom," in order to avoid the pantheistic connotation of "Namaste" and related greetings in other languages of India. In forms of explicit pantheism, the greatest fulfillment one can hope for is to lose personal identity to the greatness of the divine whole, like a drop of water falling into the great ocean. Many North Americans and Europeans gravitate toward a pantheistic way of thinking without realizing it, such as trains of thought in the direction of the universe being a creative force of its own, or eternally pre-existent. Pantheistic thought also tends toward the worship of nature and preservationist environmentalism which seeks to preserve nature for its own sake (contrasted with conservationism, which seeks to preserve nature for the responsible use and enjoyment of present and future human generations.) When the Apologist hears these types of comments from the unbeliever along these lines, he can safely put them in the pantheist category. The key point of emphasis for the Apologist with all pantheistic types of thinking will be creation. Creation as recorded in the Bible makes a hard distinction between the Creator and His creation. This is known as the Creator/creature distinction. The creation reflects its Creator, and He fills it, but it is not He, nor can it contain Him.

c. Polytheism—Greek, Norse, Wicca, animism.

Polytheism is the belief in multiple gods. It prevailed among ancient peoples with various lists of gods worshipped by the Egyptians, Greeks and Romans, Celts, and Germanic tribes. Pantheism posits an impersonal divine force that is the universe. Polytheism often comes along with it in various forms, since man craves an object of worship that he can personally relate to. This is why in pantheistic Hinduism, many individual personal manifestations are worshipped. The Hindu in India will acknowledge a pantheistic view of the universe with expressions like, "god is one", while at the same time bowing down to individual rocks daubed in orange paint in shrines found scattered around the city, and keeping one special room for his household idol in his tiny house built with mud walls. Although pantheism tends to the worship of nature in general, the human being craving personal devotion to deity will identify individual manifestations of nature as specific gods, such as the Norse god of thunder, Thor, and the Greek Poseidon, god of the ocean. So, expressions of polytheism often accompany pantheistic beliefs. Polytheist spirituality is commonly marked by obsession with human sex or perverse eroticism and worship of nature. Some modern revivalists of explicit polytheistic devotion are attempting to reconnect with an ancient cultural heritage, like nostalgic instances of devotion to Zeus in modern Greece or some of the Odinists I encountered when I was working in a prison as chaplain, who were promoting a Nordic cultural and racial identity. But more widespread today are forms of neo- pagan spirituality that glorify erotic perversion like "same sex marriage" and extreme forms of preservationist environmentalism like celebrations of the neo-pagan holiday "earth day" and the purchase of *carbon credits*, the modern form of indulgences purchased to atone for ones sins against "Mother Nature." For the purposes of the conversational Apologist, you will appropriately respond to explicit polytheistic claims when they arise in the form of claims of multiple gods, whether sincere or when the unbeliever is playing devil's advocate. Claims of polytheism are not significantly more difficult for the Apologist to disprove than those of the materialistic naturalist or the pantheist. The answer that many personal gods shaped the universe as we know it begs many of the same questions that those other worldviews do.

d. "Abrahamic faiths"

I put the term "Abrahamic faiths" in parentheses because this category refers not to those who genuinely follow in the footsteps of faithful Abraham, who are believers in the Lord Jesus

Christ as He is revealed in the Holy Scriptures from Genesis through Revelation, but a category that includes all those who claim to worship the God of Abraham. Into this category fall such faiths as modern Judaism and Islam, and heretical forms of Christianity like Roman Catholicism, Mormonism, Jehovah's Witnesses, and Seventh Day Adventism. The procedure for countering the false claims of such belief systems is quite clear, since they all in some way affirm the authenticity of at least a part of the Holy Scriptures. So the task of the Apologist in this case will be to show how the books of Holy Scripture (that these groups acknowledge as authentic) are inconsistent with their claims about the God of Abraham or other foundational doctrines of theirs. The Apologist will in this case put careful effort into explaining the Scriptures to show that they confirm the doctrines confessed by orthodox Protestant churches, especially those of the Reformed

Churches.

Chapter II: How to defend the faith vs. Atheism

As we proceed to look at examples of how to defend biblical Christianity against competing philosophical worldviews, let us first examine Atheism. We are going to assume that the Atheist in this case is a materialistic naturalist—one who denies the existence of supernatural phenomena, as is most common. While there are some out there who have a belief that there is no God while at the same time believing in ghosts and the like, this type of view tends toward pantheism, or polytheism, or both, and so, where such peculiar views arise the Apologist may judge what is the best way to defend against them.

A. Laws of morality

The laws of morality prove the existence of the Trinitarian God of Scripture, because no other philosophical worldview can rationally account for their existence. That is, no other view explains how there can be unchanging, universal, objective laws of morality. This can come up in conversation in one of the following ways.

Atheist: "I believe that the important thing is to be a good person and empathize with fellow human beings. As long as you do that, no god is needed."

The Atheist is making a claim for a standard of morality. His proclamation of it to the Christian implies that he thinks it applies universally, or at least beyond himself. Furthermore he has just made a universal statement regarding universal laws of the universe, based on his notion of what the standard of morality should be. The Christian answers in the following way,

Christian: "I understand that you think empathy toward other human beings should be the universal standard of morality. Your statement at least suggests that. I'm a Christian, and my Bible teaches me to have compassion on other human beings because they are image-bearers of God. On the other hand, how do you, as an atheist, account for the existence of universal laws of morality at all?"

Atheist: "Account for? What does that mean? It's right to empathize with other human beings. Everyone knows that."

Christian: "Actually not everyone agrees on that. Throughout history many nations have considered it a virtue to kill people of rival nations or tribes, etc. By *account for*, I simply mean, how, given your atheistic worldview, can there be such a thing as universal,

47

unchanging laws of morality?"

Atheist: "I just know that it's right to empathize with other human beings. Who says I have to 'account for' anything? I don't have to. And what is all this talk about my 'atheistic worldview?' I don't even have a philosophical worldview. I just don't see evidence for a god."

Christian: "When you empathize with other human beings, you show the image of your Creator, the Trinitarian God of Scripture, written on your heart. You are selectively borrowing from my biblical Christian worldview when you do that. By 'atheistic worldview', I just mean your framework for understanding reality as a whole, as an atheist."

Atheist: "I do no such thing! I'm not borrowing from any religion, certainly not Christianity."

Christian: "I assert that you are, unless and until you can account for the existence of universal laws of morality."

Atheist: "I don't believe in universal laws of morality. I think societies developed the principles of empathy over millions of years in order to preserve human life and live together peacefully."

Christian: "So the principle of empathy evolved? So it must still be evolving."

Atheist: "Yes, it evolved. And sure, I think we are making progress in understanding empathy for other human beings all the time."

Christian: "If that were true, we couldn't even be having this conversation about morality. My

49

morality may be more evolved than yours, or less evolved than yours. There is no universal standard of morality in that case. Your standard: *empathy* is entirely subjective and arbitrary. You can't prove to me that it is the universal standard applying in all times to all people everywhere, can you? What about people who think it's right to kill human beings in order to save the earth and stop pollution? Can you prove them wrong?"

Atheist: "Um…"

Christian: "Exactly. When you value human life, and I'm glad you do, you show the image of God written on your heart. But it conflicts with your stated worldview. Did you notice that you couldn't even begin to account for the existence of a universal standard of right and wrong? You suggested empathy as the standard, but you have no rational philosophical basis for saying it's always right for me to have compassion on other human beings. You're not wrong about that, but your worldview can't account for it. May I suggest that you exchange your irrational worldview, that doesn't begin to account for basic moral principles that you know intuitively, and embrace biblical Christianity instead? In this way you will be able to rationally account for the existence of universal laws of morality, including the requirement to empathize with other human beings, because they are created by God after His own image. The Lord Jesus is merciful to receive everyone who repents of his sin and submits to Him in faith."

At this point, if the Atheist has anything more to say, he will change the subject, or signal defeat by attacking you personally. You have confronted the irrationality of his worldview when it comes to accounting for the universal principles of morality that he himself knows intuitively, and offered an alternative way of thinking, one conformed to God's revelation in the Holy Scriptures. You can point out that he is resorting to an *ad hominem* fallacy, a tactic of last resort, and pivot to the gospel.

Or, the topic of morality may come up in conversation this way,

Atheist: "In the Bible God commands the Israelites to exterminate the Canaanites, including women and children. This is morally reprehensible. I cannot worship such a wicked God."

Christian: "There's a good reason why God commanded them to do that[6], but first of

---

[6] Deuteronomy 20:16ff.

all, let me ask a basic question. By what standard are you judging God's command to be immoral?"

Atheist: "What do you mean 'by what standard?' Come on, killing innocent women and children?"

Christian: "There is no one innocent. But let me rephrase the question more precisely, how, in your worldview, can you account for universal laws of morality?"

Atheist: "They don't exist."

Christian: "Forgive me, but it sure seemed like you believed in universal laws of morality when you were criticizing God's command to kill the Canaanites. How can such laws exist, in a universe without God?"

Atheist: "Well, I mean, it was a terrible thing to do, killing those people."

Christian: "Terrible by what standard? Can you prove it?"

Atheist: "Prove it? It's just the way I feel about it."

Christian: "I understand that feeling, but your worldview doesn't offer any rational account for the existence of the kind of moral standard that you're attempting to apply to my God. It's entirely subjective and arbitrary. In fact, if it were not for the Trinitarian God of Scripture, we couldn't even be having a conversation right now about the morality of Israel killing the Canaanites. The very notion of moral laws would be utterly meaningless. We might as well be shouting gibberish at each other. When you affirm universally applicable standards of morality, you selectively borrow from the biblical Christian worldview. You intuitively know that there are moral laws from God's creation, but your atheistic worldview can't account for them. You might consider exchanging it for biblical Christianity, which is the only rational worldview that can account for basic truths of our reality, like universal laws of morality. And we can discuss why God gave that command."

Or, the subject of moral law may come up like this,

Atheist: "Children are raped every day in this world. If God is truly in control, he must be very evil to allow this to go on. What kind of god would have the power to stop child rape and yet permit it to happen daily around the world?"

Christian: "You bring up what are horrible sins and crimes. We don't have all the answers when it comes to difficult questions like these, but in faith we accept that God has ordained all of the sorrows and atrocities of this life for an ultimately good purpose. But, on the other hand, your worldview offers no rationally consistent basis for a universal moral law prohibiting the sin of child rape. Our God has very strictly prohibited such crimes against little ones in His word."

Atheist: "There are no universal laws of morality. We've just developed guidelines for behavior that will help humanity to thrive."

Christian: "Ok. Cool. Pardon me while I empty your bank account electronically."

Atheist: "Ha-ha. Good one. But that would be something that would adversely impact me, so you can't do it."

Christian: "Why not?"

Atheist: "Because it's against the law."

Christian: "So, I think it's an unjust law, like the Jim Crow laws during segregation. Sometimes there are unjust laws, and people have to take action, do you agree?"

Atheist: "Yes, but not that one. That's theft."

Christian: "Yes, and I'm Robin Hood. My theft is justified because you have too much money in your account."

Atheist: "Society has long held that theft is wrong."

Christian: "So, why should I care about that? If I can get away with it, prove to me that I shouldn't electronically empty your bank account."

Atheist: "I'm not telling you what you should do, I'm just describing what society says about it."

Christian: "Why is that of any concern to me? I'm going to be extra careful not to get caught. Do you see how, in this scenario, you were not able to account for the most basic laws of morality? Even if you have never been taught, you know the commandment of God, 'thou shalt not steal,' and you care about children. When you do these things, you show the law of God written on your heart from creation. But your philosophical worldview can't account for them. That's an irrational worldview. It can't account for basic things about our universe, like the universal laws of morality prohibiting the rape of children or the theft of money. Embrace biblical Christianity, and then you'll be able to think rationally about moral issues like these."

In each of these hypothetical conversations, the Atheist is bringing up the subject of morality as either affirming atheism, or damaging the claims of biblical Christianity. Here is the opportunity to question the Atheist's rational consistency regarding morality. He is assuming universal, constant laws of morality. This is evident, because he is attempting to apply a standard to the Christian or to the Bible that seems right to him personally. By applying it beyond himself, and even to consideration of the morality of the teachings of the Bible, he shows that he thinks his standard is universally applicable, not merely subjective. But his stated naturalistic worldview cannot account for any such thing as universal laws of morality. Only biblical Christianity can.

B. Laws of logic

The laws of logic are fertile ground for demonstrating the truth of the Trinitarian God of Scripture over and against atheism, because every word uttered in meaningful human communication must adhere to them. So they quickly become relevant in any conversation at all. This is personally one of my favorite topics upon which to defend the faith, because every conversation assumes the laws of logic. One tactic that I have used when atheists try and ask for data points of evidence supporting the claims of YHWH is to refer them directly to their question as evidence that He exists. Their even asking for evidence for God is proof that He exists. Why? The request for evidence presupposes the existence of the laws of logic, for example, the law of non-contradiction. The law of non-contradiction stated in terms of formal logic is expressed thusly:

$$A \neq \text{Not } A$$

Something is not both true and false at the same time, in the same way. What does the atheist's request for evidence rest on, if not an assumption that God cannot exist and not exist simultaneously? The law of non-contradiction, one of the bedrock laws of logic, dictates that God must exist or not, but that He cannot both exist and not exist. On this law, the Christian apologist and the atheist are agreed. But the Christian can account for the existence of this law of logic. There is a God who created the universe, in whom is no lie or contradiction, according to Holy Scripture. His creation reflects His attributes, including His utter truthfulness, and so in the universe that He made, something cannot exist and not exist at the same time. Nor can anything be both true and false at the same time, in the same way. The Christian knows in this way, what the origin and cause of the law of non- contradiction are. The atheist uses the law constantly in everyday life, knowing that in this universe something and its direct opposite cannot both be true at the same time in the same manner. But he knows it intuitively, and his stated worldview, atheistic materialistic naturalism, cannot even begin to explain how such a universally applicable, constant law can exist in a hypothetical godless universe. The conversation will often go something like this:

Atheist: "Show me evidence for any god."

Christian: "Well, for starters, your request for 'evidence for any god' is proof undeniable that my God YHWH exists.

Atheist: "What are you talking about? I don't believe in your God. Show me evidence that He exists or I will conclude that you're engaging in merely wishful thinking."

Christian: "No, seriously, your request is evidence for YHWH, the Trinitarian God of Holy Scripture."

Atheist: "How?"

Christian: "When you ask for evidence that YHWH exists, you do not state, but you assume that He cannot both exist and not exist at the same time, correct?"

Atheist: "Well, ya, so?"

Christian: "Your request relies upon and presupposes the existence of the law of non-contradiction as universally applicable. Do you know where the law of non-contradiction comes from?"

Atheist: "Actually I do, but go ahead and enlighten me."

Christian: "The law of non-contradiction is a product of the mind of the Trinitarian God. In Him is no lie or contradiction. So naturally this attribute of God is reflected in His creation in the form of the universal and constant law of non-contradiction. That's how we Bible-believing Christians account for it. On the other hand, you as an atheist have no way to account for the existence of the universal, constant law of non-contradiction, do you?"

Atheist: "I sure do. It evolved with the mind of man. We tend to think in specific categories or lines that have evolved through a process of trial and error known as natural selection. The law of non-contradiction was advantageous to the survival of the species, and the result is that it's embedded in our brains that something cannot be both true and not true at the same time in the same way."

Christian: "So, if it evolved, then it's still evolving."

Atheist: "No, the evolution of the law of non-contradiction in human thinking is terminal and applies universally to *homo sapiens*."

Christian: "How would you know if its evolution were terminal? Have you interviewed every single human being to verify that the law of non-contradiction is still valid?

Atheist: "Um, no…"

Christian: "In fact, it is likely still evolving, if it evolved as you said. I may have a form of logic in my mind that is more evolved than yours, or vice-versa. One of us may have discovered that something can be both true and not true at the same time in the same way, and therefore, you have no warrant to even request evidence delineating whether YHWH exists or not, since this assumes He cannot both exist and not exist at the same time."

Atheist: "OK, well, it's obvious that He cannot both exist and not exist at the same time in the same sense."

Christian: "It's only obvious because we live in the universe that YHWH created. Otherwise, there's no way of accounting for the obvious fact that something cannot be both true and not true at the same time in the same sense. When you assume that, you're borrowing from biblical Christianity again. You do that because it works in this universe. That's proof, by the way, that YHWH created it. On the other hand, your atheistic worldview has no rational way of accounting for the existence of a universal and unchanging law of non-contradiction. If your atheistic worldview were correct in reality, there could be no laws of logic. We couldn't even be having this conversation right now. Talk would be meaningless, and communication would be impossible. We might as well be shouting 'yabadabadoo' at each other. We certainly could not be having a meaningful discussion."

Atheist: "Well…"

Christian: "Give up your irrational thinking by embracing the Trinitarian God: Father, Son, and Holy Spirit, and logic! He is gracious and willing to pardon all who come through His Son Jesus Christ, even of the sin of atheism."

C. Laws of Mathematics

Once the Christian defender of the faith grasps the concept that only biblical Christianity can give a rational account for the existence of any universal, unchanging laws that govern the universe and the things in it, this principle may be applied to any universal, constant laws that man knows by observation: whether of mathematics, physics, biology, etc. One may engage in this way:

Christian: "As an atheist, you cannot even know with certainty that 2 + 2 = 4. As a Christian, I can account for the law of mathematics reflected in this equation."

Atheist: "Huh? How could it equal anything else?"

Christian: "It's hard for us to imagine the answer being anything else, inhabiting as we do God's universe, isn't it? But the law of mathematics: 2 + 2 = 4, and that it does not equal not 4, is not a material entity. It exists and governs the material things in our world, but it is itself a universal, unchanging, immaterial entity. I know that you recognize this law. You wouldn't be able to do basic math without it. But how, as an Atheist, do you account for it?"

Atheist: "I do not account for it. I simply know it

from observation."

Christian: "I'm sure that you have observed it, but have you observed every single possible instance of it? In other words, have you checked in every part of the universe to see if it is universally true everywhere?"

Atheist: "No, I have not. But it has been true every time I've observed it."

Christian: "So, by not observing every possible instance of the equation, you can't rationally conclude that it is true everywhere based on your very limited observation, can you? Have you tried solving the same equation on the moon?"

Atheist: "No, but, we couldn't even do math without it."

Christian: "You're making my point. You can't do math without the law of addition, because you inhabit the universe YHWH created. He is a rational God and He governs His universe by consistent laws such as the laws of mathematics. You know this intuitively, but since you cannot explain how it can exist in this universe, your entire view of the universe is thus demonstrated to be false. Give up on your irrational atheistic worldview and embrace biblical Christianity. Then you will have a view of things that is consistent with the way they are observed to be in reality."

Atheist: "Hmmmmm."

D. Laws of Physics

Christian: "The evidence for the existence of the Trinitarian God of Scripture is that you are sitting there in your chair."

Atheist: "What!? How is my sitting in my chair evidence for your particular Deity?"

Christian: "Because it presupposes the existence of a constant, universal law of gravity."

Atheist: "My sitting here in my chair is observable quite well enough without any reference to your God."

Christian: "That's an unproven bare assertion. I contend that you are observing it because my God exists. I assert for rational reasons that you sitting there in that chair is in fact proof of the existence of my God."

Atheist: "And how can that be?"

Christian: "Because God governs the universe by consistent laws. He sets the bodies in motion, and no one can stop them. That includes the gravitational pull of the earth on your finite material body."

Atheist: "I don't believe in your God."

Christian: "Yes, so you've said, but how do you account for the law of gravity that holds you down in that chair, aside from any reference to him?"

Atheist: "Well, I don't account for it, I just observe it."

Christian: "That is a true statement. And since you cannot account for it, I submit that means that your philosophical worldview of atheistic materialistic naturalism is utterly irrational, since it cannot account for the basic reality of the law of gravity governing this universe. On the other hand, Christianity does account for it rationally as I noted previously. Do you know why that is? There's only one answer to that question. It's because the claims of biblical Christianity about the universe are true."

E. Laws of Biology

1. General principles

Christian: "If it were not for the existence of YHWH, the stem on this blossoming, aromatic red lion in this pot wouldn't be green as you see that it is."

Atheist: "That's your claim. Got any proof?"

Christian: "Yes, of course. I wouldn't make a statement I couldn't prove to be true. The process of photosynthesis works predictably and universally on earth, temperature and other geological conditions permitting, of course.

Atheist: "Well, yes, that is a biological observation."

Christian: "Yes, but how, in your worldview, do you account for universal, unchanging laws of photosynthesis?

Atheist: "Science has yet to discover the origin of these things. Again, we simply know this by observation."

Christian: "Exactly, and do you know why you can't account for their origin? It's because your worldview: atheistic materialistic naturalism, isn't true. It colors all your thinking, but you can't account for the origin or existence of any universal, unchanging law by it. Give up your irrational worldview and embrace biblical Christianity. The Bible teaches that there is a God who created all the plants, and governs them consistently by consistent laws to provide oxygen for the earth so that humans and animals can breathe, to provide shelter, clothing, and food as well. It alone can account for the existence of this law of photosynthesis."

2. Countering claims of evidence for evolution, missing biblical flood

Quite often the atheist will raise the evolution of species as a factoid or data point that supposedly undermines the credibility of the Holy Scriptures with reference to reality. But this theory of the origin of life is a really weak challenge to the Christian worldview. It has major gaps that it cannot explain, such as the lack of transitional forms in the fossil record, and the lack of a demonstrated constructive mechanism of genetic mutation that could turn simple living molecules into a living man. The mutations that have been observed are destructive, not constructive. These gaps are so enormous that it is hard to imagine any self-respecting scientist holding to the theory, except that for the atheistic materialistic naturalist, there is no other option. No other theories of origins will satisfy his atheistic worldview. As has been previously demonstrated, the claims of evolution to explain many basic facts about our reality are very irrational indeed, like we saw with the notion that the laws of morality and laws of logic evolved.

Sometimes the atheist will raise a purported lack of evidence for the Noahic flood as a counterpoint against the accuracy of the biblical Christian worldview.

Atheist: "If the Bible is true, why isn't there evidence for a global flood?"

Christian: "A lot of work has been done in geology showing evidence for a global flood, like for example in the Grand Canyon. In addition, there are on earth over 4,000 flood stories that various nations have preserved in their oral and/or written traditions.

How do you begin to account for all that collective memory if it does not go back to a worldwide flood that actually occurred, the one recorded in Genesis 9?"

Atheist: "But the flood narrative in the epic of Gilgamesh predates the Bible, and has obvious similarities. Probably the author of Genesis copied from that story."

Christian: "The epic of Gilgamesh and other flood narratives got their story from Noah, who (along with his three daughters-in-law,) is the common ancestor of all surviving human beings. I do not dispute that the text of the epic of Gilgamesh predates the text of Scripture. But the oral tradition of the Noahic flood predates both writings."

At this point in the conversation, instead of continuing long evidential lines, I would pivot back to a presuppositional approach and demonstrate how only the presupposition of the existence of

YHWH can account for reality as we know it to be as in the case of laws of morality, logic, mathematics, empirical sciences, etc.

F. The text and transmission of the Holy Scriptures

1. Internal evidence of divine authorship in the text of Scripture

The sixty-six books of Holy Scripture are in fact the best and most clear proof for God. Do not allow the atheist or other skeptic to summarily dismiss the Bible as evidence with silly statements like "It's the claim, not evidence." A collection of sixty-six books may very well contain both claims and evidence supporting those claims, as the Bible does. Note: we are not arguing that God is true simply because the Bible makes that claim. That would be fallacious circular reasoning. We are presenting the internal evidence for the divine authorship of the Bible as proof that its claims are true, especially its claims about the Trinitarian God. There are many varied approaches that may be taken to presenting the Bible as evidence for the existence of the Trinitarian God. It is okay to venture into a defense of the truth of the Bible based on its internal, objective marks of divine authorship: the consent of its parts in one law and one gospel by over forty authors over many centuries; the scope of the whole, which is the glory of God and not of man, (no human authors write so self-deprecatingly); and especially its divine good news of salvation, which is something that no human being could ever originate, exalting God as the Author and Finisher of salvation and humbling prideful man by giving him no contributing factor in his salvation. I will often refer to these marks of divine authorship in conversation with unbelievers. But this is not, strictly speaking, a presuppositional approach. The presuppositional approach to defending the truth of Scripture would be along the lines previously discussed, demonstrating that the truth of the Bible is a necessary presupposition to any discussion of morality, logic, empirical science, and so on. The apologist will use a variety of approaches to demonstrate how the Bible proves the existence of YHWH.

The textual record of the transmission of the Scriptures is often held forth by the ignorant atheist in an attempt to undermine their testimony. The less informed may say something like,

> Atheist: "How can you trust the Bible we have today? It's been translated so many times."
>
> Christian: "The best translations translate only one time, since they go back to the original Hebrew Old Testament and Greek New Testament originals and translate directly into

English or another modern language."

Atheist: "But I read a book somewhere that says the King James Version has many differences with the oldest texts that exist."

Christian: "You're referring to issues with the transmission of the text. Any time a book in ancient times was hand-copied many times, before the invention of the printing press, minor variations resulted. The King James Version is a faithful translation into early modern English, based on the best texts they had available at the time in the original languages. But we are not limited to that translation. Our churches require that ordained ministers be proficient in the original languages of Hebrew and Greek so that they may prepare sermons and lessons based on the original text of Scripture. The variations you mention between certain early volumes like the Codex Sinaiticus and the textual basis of the King James translation are so minimal that, even when modern English translations have been made largely dependent on the Codex Sinaiticus and a couple other early codices, a denomination may allow different churches to use their preferred translation, for example the King James Version or the New American Standard, and there are no divisive doctrinal differences resulting from the use of these different translations. Furthermore, the fact that there are well over five thousand[7] complete or partial New Testament Greek manuscripts from diverse centuries and geographic sources means that we have a full record of the transmission of the text that allows us to determine what the original text said by

---

[7] Bruce Metzger and Bart Ehrman, "The Text of the New Testament", 4th ed., New York: Oxford University Press, 2005, 52.

comparing different manuscripts. No one person ever had control of all the manuscripts. In other words, there was never a theoretical opportunity to corrupt all of them. They spread out quickly from the source and were promulgated throughout the known world rapidly, in such a way that copyist mistakes can easily be ascertained by comparing individual manuscripts with the whole body of existing New Testament manuscripts that have been discovered from a diversity of sources. The textual basis of the Old Testament has been disputed very little, and was in the last century confirmed to a great extent by the discovery of some old scrolls known as the Dead Sea Scrolls."

Atheist: "But how do we know the testimony of the writers of the original text of Scripture is accurate?"

Christian: "Liars are not martyrs. Of the men who penned the New Testament by inspiration of the Holy Ghost, most of them sealed their testimony in their own blood. Liars and martyrs are not cut from the same cloth."

Atheist: "But what of scholars who say that many of the books of the New Testament were written at a much later date, and not by the reputed authors?"

Christian: "There are many textual markers and evidences in the New Testament of a first century date for them. Also, the internal, verbal evidence for the authorship of the books is weighty, and so is the testimony of the early church, which recorded histories of who wrote each book. That testimony is not infallible, but it certainly is of greater weight than the speculations of liberal scholars with an ax to grind against the doctrine of the New Testament, living nearly two millennia after it was written. We have our own history in the Church of who wrote the books, which is far more credible than the opinions of twentieth century historical revisionists."

Atheist: "But what about all the contradictions in the Bible?"

Christian: "No contradiction has ever been proven to exist in the text of the Holy Scriptures. There are a few difficult verses, but there are plausible ways of explaining each. Besides, ninety percent of the claims of contradiction that you find on popular atheist blogs and websites are so spurious, so easy to explain as a non-contradiction, that most children in our Sunday School wouldn't have trouble responding to them in a logical way that shows the harmony of the texts in question."

In the foregoing conversation, the Christian is presenting an apologetic taking an evidential and not a presuppositional approach to defending the integrity of the existing text of the Holy Scriptures. This would seem to me to be warranted, considering the impressive evidence for the purity of the text of Scripture, and the fact that it is after all a visible, tangible, testable text that is in question: the Bible itself. A presuppositional approach would highlight how the Bible provides in its teaching on God, creation, sin, and revelation, the only rationally defensible account for many things that we know in reality. But the presupposition of the Bible as the external point of contact that makes all other knowledge possible and rationally defensible rests on the assumption that God gave the Bible, that it has a consistent and coherent message, that it is one book, that its most basic claims of history and authorship are truthful, etc. The one defending the Christian faith is free to make use of different types of apologetic arguments as seems best in a given situation, in this case evidential or presuppositional arguments alternatively. And in my judgment it often makes sense to lay the intellectual foundation for the internal evidence of the text of Scripture alongside the presuppositional approach.

2. The starting point

Atheist: "If, as you have stated, Kant discovered that without an external point of reference, we are trapped in a prison of subjectivity, relying only on what our senses tell us, with no objective information on the reality around us, then how do you, as a Christian, escape that?

We are all in the same boat in that regard. You say that you have a book revealed from God as an external point of reference, but even that requires you to use your sense of sight to read and comprehend it. How do you know that you are even reading it with precise correctness, before you begin to understand it? Your sense could hypothetically be deceiving you and filtering out or distorting the real letters on the page and other stuff like that. How do you know that you can trust your senses when you use them to read the Bible any more than I do when I'm independently examining natural evidence? Aren't we both in the same boat, trusting our sense and ability to reason?"

Christian: "The answer is that in the grace of regeneration, a miracle of God, when he gave me a new heart for the old one, and turned my blindness into sight, has given me a full confidence that the words my eyes see in the text of Scripture are the very word of God. The external became communicated to me internally, not in the form of new revelation, but in confirming the truth of the testimonies that are contained in Scripture, by the Holy Spirit, when He opened my eyes."

Atheist: "But how do you know that your eyes have been opened?"

Christian: "How do you know that the light switch has been turned on in your bedroom, or that your lens prescription is correct, if you wear glasses? You know because you can see clearly what is there in front of you. In the same way I know that my eyes have been opened to clearly perceive and believe the truths written in the testimony of the Bible because through them I see reality as it truly is.

When you are in a dark room, you may have vague and speculative notions about what is in the room, but once the light has been turned on, you cannot go back to incorrect notions about what the layout of the furniture is. The clarity of the perception attests to reality. So it is with the Scriptures, for one that has been born again, which is a sovereign act of the Holy Spirit upon him. He sees reality clearly in Scripture as a mirror, and he can no longer deny the claims that it makes about it."

G. The argument from ignorance

Occasionally if you are debating a really astute atheist, he may say that your accounting for basic laws and facts in a hypothetical way via the biblical testimony does not preclude the possibility that there may be a more correct worldview that would account for all of these things while holding to atheism, that perhaps has just not yet been discovered. He is logically correct. In theory, you have not exhausted every possible worldview. You have only exhausted every conceivable worldview. But the rational defense of Christianity through the presuppositional method that we have conducted, while not technically watertight in the philosophical sense, is nonetheless a compelling challenge to the stated worldview of the atheist (or any unbeliever.) You have demonstrated the utter irrationality of him being an atheist while not being able to account for basic facts about our reality, and you have demonstrated biblical Christianity to be, at least, the only rationally defensible system of thought that can currently be conceived of. That is compelling proof indeed.

Chapter III: How to defend the faith vs. Pantheism

Pantheism, again, is the belief that the entire universe is itself an impersonal divine force, and that everything in it partakes of the divine essence. All of the same irrationalities that have been demonstrated in the materialistic naturalist worldview that most atheists hold to are present in pantheism as well. Pantheism cannot give a rational account for the existence of constant, universal laws, whether of morality, logic, mathematics, or the empirical sciences. It asserts that these things simply always were, those constant and universal laws that govern the universe. The law of causality recognized since Aristotle states that in this universe, every effect must have a cause[8]. The cause of the universe, therefore, cannot be itself, since that would simply kick the causality can down the road. The universe that is governed by laws cannot itself

[8] Holzamer, 205.

be the cause of those laws, or they would be inferior to it, not governing it. Since the law of causality governs the universe, implied by the fact that it governs everything observed in the universe, therefore, the universe is not the cause of such universal laws. So it lacks a rational explanation for the existence of a law like for example, the law of non-contradiction, and the same kind of dialogue used with the atheist may be applied.

Pantheist: "The whole universe is one eternal, self-sustaining power. The more we can be one with what is outside ourselves, the more enlightened we will be."

Christian: "Oh, really? Is this governed by the law of gravity?"

Pantheist: "Yes. That is a clearly observable attribute of it. We can assume it has been that way from all eternity."

Christian: "My Bible teaches me that the Trinitarian God: Father, Son, and Holy Spirit, created the entire universe in a timespan of six days. He set the bodies in motion, and because He governs this universe consistently, the law of gravity never changes, and we can rely on it when making astronomical calculations etc."

Pantheist: "God is not distinct from the universe. The universe is god."

Christian: "If that is true, then how do you account for the existence of the law of gravity? If it governs the universe, it has not its origin in the universe."

Pantheist: "Well, I'm not sure how to explain that."

Christian: "I can. As I explained before, the Trinitarian God who created this universe governs it consistently. You cannot explain how the law of gravity exists through the lens of your worldview because it does not reflect reality. When you say that the universe is god, you are erasing the important distinction between the Creator and His creation. Repent of your irrational pantheism, and embrace biblical Christianity. Our Lord Jesus is gracious and merciful to accept all who come to the Father through Him, the Creator. He made you after His own image, not to be erased as to your individuality, but to be a tiny, finite reflection of Him, worshipping and glorifying Him forever."

Rational thinking about the universe requires also that the law of causality that governs it be accounted for.

Christian: "The law of causality, that every effect has a cause, proves the existence of YHWH."

Pantheist: "How does it do that?"

Christian: "The law of causality exists in the universe, meaning that every effect has a cause. This law in fact points back to the First Cause. You see, in this universe, there is a law of causality governing causes and effects, because when, as the Bible teaches us, YHWH created everything that exists, in other words, the universe, He Himself was that Uncaused Cause. The law of causality cannot apply to Him, precisely because of the important distinction between the Creator and the creature. He is not a part of the universe, and is not bound by its laws. The Creator is uncaused. The Creature is caused, and in it everything has a cause. This is how we know that the universe is caused. And, as God tells us in Genesis, He Himself is that First Cause. On the other hand, your worldview is irrational, since it can't account for the existence of the law of causality that governs it, as previously demonstrated."

Chapter IV: How to defend the faith vs. Polytheism

Polytheism in various forms and manifestations posits that there are many gods controlling and sustaining reality as we know it. These gods are finite beings, created themselves, but with powers and knowledge above what humans possess. As a result, all of the same things that cause problems for the atheist are also unaccounted for by the polytheist. He cannot explain the origin or existence of universal laws, whether for morality, logic, or physics, for these laws also govern his gods. In effect, man has created gods after his own image. He cannot account for the law of causality at play in the universe, for his gods are also caused.

He can point to the origin of human life with myths like that of the Norse frost giant Ymir, who gave birth to mankind, supposedly, a male and a female from each respective armpit[9], but this begs the question of where the great frost giant came from (leaving aside the absurdity of the myth.) So, all of the irrationalities of materialistic naturalism and pantheism also apply to the worldview of the polytheist. His worldview lacks the creative unity of one Creator God. It cannot account for the unity of the universe. In the universe there is diversity, and there is unity. There are many bodies, but there are unified laws of motion that govern all, and consistent properties between bodies of like mass and matter. There is a unity of the whole that pervades all. The decadent lore of competing deities creating, building, destroying, or misbehaving in the cosmos often after the example of the worst of mankind offers no rational account for the unifying principles of reality in the universe that we inhabit. How do a group of sometimes warring, always scheming gods sustain a universe consistently and predictably? The polytheist

---

[9] *Poetic Edda.*

cannot answer this question. If his worldview were correct, we would be constantly in danger of up being down and down being up based on the latest squabble between deities.

Christian: "How do you account for unchanging, universal laws of logic?"

Polytheist: "The pantheon that I worship, on Mount Olympus, has made a pact that these laws of existence will consistently govern the affairs of men."

Christian: "So, what would happen if one, let's say Hades, that mischievous deity, were to rebel and change the laws of logic, so that both A and not A can be true simultaneously, for the people who are temporarily under his control."

Polytheist: "Well, we don't know. That hasn't

happened."

Christian: "How do you know that hasn't happened? Have you checked every time and location to see if maybe that had ever happened? How could you predict the actions of a rebel deity like Hades in my example, ahead of time? Your worldview does not allow for human thought to be consistently and confidently governed by the laws of logic, such as the law of non-contradiction. If this law is governed by your gods, in your worldview, then we cannot predict what course they may take, for they depend on the behavior of whimsical beings, if the Iliad and other myths are any indication. If you say the gods do not have the power to change the laws of logic, then they too, are governed by them, and you have no account at all for the existence of the laws of logic. May I humbly suggest that you give up on this irrational polytheistic view of the universe, and embrace the God of the Bible, who governs all things consistently and unchangingly, as He never changes?"

Chapter V: How to defend the faith vs. "Abrahamic" faiths

Finally, we come to the so-called Abrahamic faiths. These are those systems of thought which claim to follow the God of Abraham. With the exception of Mormonism, all of them are monotheistic. Let us proceed to show how they may be defended against one by one.

A. Judaism

Judaism was naturally the first false teaching to oppose itself to the teachings of Christianity. This refers not to the religion of the Jews from the time of Abraham, Isaac, Jacob, and Judah until Messiah came, but the unbelieving redefinition that it found after the destruction of Jerusalem by Caesar Titus in 70 A. D. After the blocks of the temple were made to tumble and the priestly Levitical genealogies destroyed, the pharisaical sect of rabbis, minus those who had put their faith in Messiah, crafted a new religion based largely on a rejection of and opposition to the claims of the Messiah, Jesus of Nazareth. Judaism became vehemently anti-Trinitarian and anti-Christian, while retaining the Hebrew Bible that prophesied of Christ. The most natural apologetic for the Christian, then, will be to elucidate the Old Testament Scriptures which point to Jesus Christ, and speak of Him. There are many resources, especially a good Bible translation with Scripture cross-references, which will aid the apologist in this task. For the purpose of this guide, I will bypass that approach and offer one that is uniquely presuppositional for the reader's consideration. The reader will not lack other resources to help him to bring Old Testament Scripture to bear in proving the claims of Jesus the Messiah.

Jew: "God is one Lord. The Trinitarian doctrine is a form of polytheism."

Christian: "The Trinity is not polytheistic. We confess one God in three Persons. However, how do you, as a Jew, account for the diversity that exists in this universe? There is one universe, with one law of gravity, one law of causality, etc., but there are many objects and forms of matter and energy contained in it. It is not one simple mass. If the creation reflects the Creator, how do you, as a monotheistic Jew believing, to use Christian terminology, that there is one god in one person, account for the fact that our universe is not one simple and consistent mass, a blob of uniform matter and energy, but a synergistic and unified compilation of a great diverse many beings, animals, plants, and bodies? The attributes of the creation reflect the attributes of the Creator.

The Bible states that there is one God in three Persons: the Father, the Son, and the Holy Spirit, and that these three are one God. That accounts for both the unity of the universe and the diversity of it, since the creation is a reflection of the unity and diversity in the Creator. But your view can't account for that diversity. Give up your irrational worldview by embracing the Holy Trinity: Father, Son, and Holy Spirit, and you will not only become rational in your thinking, you will find peace for your soul."

This same argument would work effectively in debate with someone holding to any other monolithically monotheistic worldview, such as Muslims, Deists, or Unitarians.

B. Islam

Islam is the second largest monotheistic faith by global population. It originated with an allegedly illiterate man named Muhammed in the seventh century A. D. who said he was a prophet, claimed to have a new revelation from the God of Abraham, and backed up his claims with an army of followers. Its revered book, the Qur'an, borrows many ideas from Judaism and Christianity, with unique twists. It praises Jesus (Isa, in Arabic) as a great prophet, only second to Muhammed, and calls him the Masih[10] (Messiah), a title which unhappily is left undefined. Islam runs into many of the same problems as Judaism. It also posits a Unitarian deity who is the creator of all. It cannot account for the diversity that exists in the universe, since the creation must be a reflection of the Creator.

---

[10] Qur'an, 5:75.

Only the Trinity can account for that. It runs into the same problem of Judaism, actually a bigger one, for it theoretically affirms the validity of both the Old Testament (Toraut) and New Testament (Injil), while contradicting both, for example by denying that God has a Son. It both affirms and contradicts the Old and New Testaments. This internal inconsistency makes it rationally indefensible.

Once I was traveling by air on an international flight, and happened to be sitting next to a Pakistani Muslim. We engaged in conversation, and before long, we were talking about the things of the Lord. In order to illustrate the grace of God in Christ for sinners, I brought up the account of Abraham nearly sacrificing his son (Isaac, however, Muslims believe it was Ishmael, so I was purposely vague in this instance on who the son was, to make a greater point.) I told him that just as God had provided a ram in place of Abraham's son, so God in grace had provided His own Son in place of sinners like us, to take the death that we deserve for our sins. His response let me know immediately that he got the point. He said, "But if that is true, what will prevent people from doing all kinds of wicked things?" In other words, his works-righteousness mindset led him to think that only the fear of eternal punishment can make people obedient, that unconditional forgiveness in Christ is a license to sin. Paul asked[11] hypothetically, "Shall we continue in sin, that grace may abound?" Of course the answer was, "God forbid. For how may we, who are dead to sin, live any longer therein?" The carnal man, upon hearing that his sins may be forgiven freely, thinks immediately that all restraint of sin is gone. But the born-again believer, loving God, and genuinely thankful for His grace, seeks to serve Him with renewed obedience. Grace and assurance of

---

[11] Romans 6:1,2.

pardon are important themes to iterate with Muslims in addition to the internal inconsistencies of the claims of Islam noted before.

Chapter VI: How to defend the faith vs. Christian heresies

A. Roman Catholicism

Roman Catholicism would not be very difficult to debunk based on the Scriptures, except that its proponents have artfully crafted a number of deceitful arguments over the centuries since the Protestant Reformation to justify the claims of the Church of Rome. The arguments of the Protestant Reformers and their direct descendants remain valid. Indeed, all that is really needed to counter the claims of Roman Catholicism is a thorough knowledge of the Scriptures in its core doctrines. The biggest departures of Roman Catholicism are in the areas of authority and the way of salvation.

Rome claims that the Church has authority to teach doctrines beyond what is taught in the Holy Scriptures. It defends this position by appealing to a claim that the Church had the authority to determine the canon, to decide what was in Holy Scripture, and the rule devised by the Church, the Holy Scriptures, therefore cannot supersede its source of authority: the Church, according to this claim. In response it is sufficient to note how Christ and the apostles used the testimony of Scripture, as authoritative to regulate the entire Church. That only the Old Testament existed in the form of a collected canon in that day, is immaterial.

The way that Christ and the apostles used existing Scripture defines the use of the completed canon for the Church today. The church councils such as the 4th century council of Carthage that listed the canon of the New Testament, did so in response to heretical movements that were seeking to remove and deny certain parts of it. There had previously been no need for the Church to make authoritative statements on what was in the canon of Holy Scripture, because the list was basically known to the whole Church since the days of the apostles, and such a pronouncement would have been of little value. It was the Scriptures that regulated and created the existence of the Church, as her foundation, not the other way around.

Roman Catholic: "Why do you not join yourself unto the true Catholic Church, instead of following after these new-fangled heresies?

Christian: "I am a part of the true Church, which is built upon the foundation of the Holy Scriptures left to us by the prophets and apostles."

Roman Catholic: "But don't you realize that it's the Catholic Church that determined the canon by the vote of councils? Without the Roman Catholic Church, you can't have a Bible. And the Bible derives its authority from the church, and that means its traditional interpretations are normative for the correct understanding of it. The authority to determine what goes into it implies the authority to definitively interpret it as well."

Christian: "First off, the Church of Rome didn't determine the canon. The Council at Carthage made up of bishops from North Africa made the first authoritative ecclesiastical (church) canon listing what the New Testament canon is, quite independently of the bishop of Rome (aka. "Pope".) Secondly, they were only stating what was already obvious to all Christians, but only came into question as a result of heresies impugning the canonicity of some of the books of the Bible. A formal list was only necessary in response to these heretics, to declare, not determine, what was already known since the days of the apostles.

The Scriptures, furthermore, are the only existing record that can be trusted of what Christ, the apostles, and prophets preached and taught, and extra-biblical traditions, which once may have carried some degree of weight, have been hopelessly corrupted. Councils and popes have developed new doctrines, and contradicted themselves, so that there is no firm evidence of any originally authentic traditions outside of what is found in the Old and New Testaments of the Holy Bible. I suggest that you take the firm and sure rock of Holy Scripture and judge every tradition that you are taught by it, and you will find that you are able to distinguish the false church from the true by that touchstone."

Roman Catholic: "But what of Luther's novel doctrine of justification? The church fathers clearly taught, in line with the apostles, that one must do good works to be saved. An external and entirely alien, imputed righteousness is a legal fiction unworthy of God. He saves, that is, He justifies, by making the sinner holy from the inside by His powerful work of grace."

Christian: "You do err, not knowing the Scriptures. For justification is a distinct grace from sanctification: God's making of His people holy. These things are never separated, but not to be confused. Whom God forgives, in Christ, he makes holy. But He does not forgive them on the basis of His making them holy, but only for the righteousness of Jesus Christ imputed to them. "But to him that worketh not, but believeth on him that justifieth the ungodly, his faith is counted for righteousness[12]." Justification is free, unmerited, and instantaneous. It belongs to the believer the

12 Romans 4:5.

moment he first repents of his sin and believes in Christ. Sanctification, God's making of His people holy, is the evidence and fruit of it, which continues and progresses throughout the Christian life. Please put down your Roman Catholic commentaries, homilies, and study notes, and read the following passages for yourself, carefully, which make this relation quite clear: Romans chapters 1-6, and the letter to the Galatians."

B. Mormonism

The Church of Jesus Christ of Latter Day Saints is a uniquely American cult started by Joseph Smith, a man from upstate New York in the early 19th century. It has grown worldwide in recent decades, and is famous for sending young men, dubbed "elders" as missionaries throughout the U. S. and abroad. Adherents, called, "Mormons", like to describe themselves as Christians. Their usual tactic is to claim to agree with orthodox Christianity on just about everything, and to attempt to avoid bringing up their stranger doctrines, like the birth of god the father on a planet near a star named Kolob[13], their hope to become gods in the celestial kingdom if they qualify through good works and temple observance, and the existence of a heavenly mother who is procreating spirit babies (all humanity and elder brothers Jesus, Lucifer) by sexual intercourse with the heavenly father. They are generally taught to engage winsomely and put a Christian veneer on Mormonism. The first task in conversation will often be to nail them down to admitting a point of disagreement with you. It could go something like this:

Christian: "Hi, I'm a believer in Jesus Christ."

---

[13] The book of Abraham 3:2-3.

Mormon: "Me, too. I'm also a believer in Jesus Christ."

Christian: "I believe in Him as He is revealed in the Bible."

Mormon: "Me, too. I also believe the Bible. But did you know that there is also another testimony of Jesus Christ?"

Christian: "No, I don't believe that. I believe the Book of Mormon to be a forgery."

Mormon: "But, why? It has the same teachings as the Bible, only clearer."

Christian: "No, it actually contradicts the Bible on such important doctrines as the total depravity of man having sinned in Adam, and

God's sovereign decree of predestination."

Mormon: "Oh, I don't believe in those things. I only accept the Bible as far as it has been correctly translated. The Book of Mormon corrects some doctrines that result from mistranslations in the King James Version."

Christian: "Now, hold on, are you competent to read Hebrew and Greek, (because our pastors are required to be able to explain the Scriptures in the original languages?)"

Mormon: "No, I am not."

Christian: "Is your bishop at your home congregation competent in Hebrew and Greek, then?"

Mormon: "No, he is a businessman who serves

the church part-time."

Christian: "How about your teachers at the Missionary Training Center?"

Mormon: "No, they didn't read Hebrew or Greek, either."

Christian: "Then you cannot even begin to logically claim that all of the major English Bible translations including the King James Version have mistranslated, can you?"

Mormon: "Well, I believe the Book of Mormon is true and some passages in the Bible have been mistranslated."

Christian: "In all major versions, in all modern languages? On what rational basis do you claim this?"

Mormon: "I had a burning in my bosom when I prayed for wisdom about the claims of the Book of Mormon, and I just know it's true!"

Christian: "I have met Muslims and Hindus who have the same kind of feelings about their gods. Does that prove their beliefs to be true? You have offered no rational basis upon which to justify your claim that the Bible has been mistranslated in passages like Romans chapter 4-5 on sin; and Ephesians chapter 1-2, and Romans chapter 9 on predestination. The testimony of Scripture is clear, and correctly translated. You will have to come to terms with the God who gave the Bible, as He is described in it, or you will perish forever in hell."

C. Seventh-Day Adventism

Another of the 19th century cults that has lived on until today is Seventh-Day Adventism. Seventh-Day Adventism claims that worship on the first day of the week is a remnant of Roman Catholicism not warranted by God. It promotes aspects of Jewish dietary law. It preaches a form of works-righteousness which is against the Bible's teaching that we are saved by grace through faith alone. It teaches a deficient view of the justice of God through its doctrine of *annihilationism,* claiming that no human beings will suffer in hell eternally for their sin, but that they will simply expire, which is nothing less than an affront to the justice of God. As Jonathan Edwards famously testified in his sermon, "God's Justice in the Damnation of Sinners", anything less than eternal punishment for sin would not fit the crime of the slightest sin committed against the infinite holiness of God. Any sin committed against Him who is infinitely worthy of obedience by a finite creature can never be fully recompensed upon that finite creature in time. A lesser punishment inflicted for sin would be beneath God's holy nature, and impugn His righteousness. A conversation with a Seventh-Day Adventist might go like this:

Seventh-Day Adventist: "Why do you worship on Sunday? Do you know that is a mark of Antichrist?"

Christian: "Because our Lord commanded it in the New Testament by good and necessary consequence, that is by logical implication, and by example[14]. Furthermore, the first day of the week is referred to as the 'Lord's Day' not only by the apostolic fathers[15], the earliest Christian

[14] John 20:1, 19, 26; Acts 20:7; 1 Corinthians 16:2.
[15] Ignatius of Antioch, "Letter to the Magnesians", *The Apostolic*

126

literature we have outside the Bible, dating to the first decade of the second Century A. D. but more importantly by the apostle John by inspiration of the Holy Spirit in the book of Revelation (1:10)."

D. Jehovah's Witnesses

Jehovah's Witnesses are another of the cults started in antebellum America, holding much in common with the ancient heresy of Arianism. With it, it holds that Christ the Son is the first creature of the father. Jehovah's Witnesses equate Him with Michael the Archangel. Of all heresies it may well be the most pernicious. It posits that man must save himself, following God's rules, in order to gain heaven. A conversation could go like this:

Fathers, Michael W. Holmes, ed., Grand Rapids, MI: Baker Books, 1992, 155.

Jehovah's Witness: "Surely you know how Christ, the Son of God, was created by the father."

Christian: "According to John chapter 1, the Word was with God, and the Word was God. The Word became flesh and dwelt among us. What am I leaving out?"

Jehovah's Witness: "Actually, the correct translation of John 1:3 is that he is 'a god.'"

Christian: "All Bible translations besides the New World Translation translate it as 'God', not: 'a god.' Careful scholarship went into all of these translations, so that your unique translation is very unlikely. Furthermore even your own translation affirms that Christ is God Himself, for example in Matthew 28:19 and Romans 9:5."

Chapter VII: Conclusion

In the foregoing pages, I have attempted to make useful and illustrative dialogues to help Christians know how to intelligently defend their faith against the objections of almost every category of unbeliever they are likely to encounter. Specific objections have been drawn from my memory of specific conversations with individuals over the years, in person or on social media, people representing many different worldviews. I spent the most time on atheism, because this growing way of thinking makes a wide variety of counterclaims to the God of the Bible, so that most of the defenses against the atheist's argument that the apologist maintains in his arsenal are also effective against other systems of thought.

Worldview example dialogues are progressively shorter because they relate only those types of arguments that have not previously been covered. I proceeded from atheism to the "Abrahamic faiths" and Christian heresies because this seemed to fit the natural flow of logic from the abstract to the more specific. The intent is that this handbook will be a useful resource for the Christian layperson to have at his fingertips, to answer almost every kind of objection effectively: a segue to the gospel. I have mainly followed the presuppositional approach, attacking the rebellious though process of the unbeliever at its root of pride in its pretended autonomy from God, its presupposition of autonomous reason, which assumes the non-existence of the Trinitarian God of the Bible right from the start. Man can only reason autonomously if the God of the Bible does not exist, and, since He does, his every thought is dependent upon God. The presupposition of autonomous reason is therefore an assumption that YHWH does not exist. In this way of arguing for the existence of the God of the Bible, a confrontation is set up with the rebellious mind of the unbeliever, and a conversational opening is made for the good news of Jesus Christ who is ready to accept them if they repent of their unbelief and submit themselves to Him. (I have only departed from a presuppositional approach briefly where it seemed appropriate.) Apologetics is not a necessary article of faith. Christians may effectively testify of Christ without it, but it helps, both in their own thinking about these issues of thought, and in conversations with unbelievers. As a Christian, you, O reader, have the intellectual resources available to you that will help you to effectively and intelligently answer any objection that enemies of Christ may level against your precious faith. May this book be a help to those who read. And, if it is not helpful, may it perish to be seen no more.

Made in the USA
San Bernardino, CA
30 July 2018